Unlocking
YOUR GIFTS
&
FINDING PURPOSE IN LIFE

MALIK K. MURRAY

Copyright © 2020 By Malik K. Murray

All rights reserved. No part of this publication may be reproduced, distributed, or transmitted in any form or by any means, including photocopying, recording, or other electronic or mechanical methods, without the prior written permission of the publisher, except in the case of brief quotations embodied in critical reviews and certain other noncommercial uses permitted by copyright law.

Images in this book are provided by ANI Portraits, Sugar Love Studio, Jeremy Bostwick, and Asya Photography.

Book Design by HMDpublishing

Dedication

This E-book is dedicated to my Family. To my very patient wife (Alissa), beautiful daughter (Addison), and observant son (Aidan), you make me become a better human being, daily. All of you teach me something new about being a husband, father, and leader.
It means a lot that God has placed each of you all in my life to challenge me for a purpose way beyond my comprehension. I am so grateful to live life with you and grow together as a family.

I truly believe that you can only be successful with the right team in place. This is my A-team. Thank you for holding me down through the good, bad, and ugly of becoming an author. Hopefully, I've made you very proud with this piece of work.

At least until I write the next book. Love you all
to the moon and back.

Contents

Introduction

Chapter 1: Assessing Who You are and the Person You are Becoming

    Why Self Reflection is Needed to Unlock Your Gifts and Find your Purpose in Life

    How to Self-Reflect

Chapter 2: Discovering Your Unique Gifts

    How to Unlock Your Unique Gift

Chapter 3: Finding Your Purpose Path

Chapter 4: Finding Hope in Your Gifts and Purpose

Chapter 5: Killing Every Fear

    How to Overcome Your Fears

Chapter 6: Holding On To Your Vision

    What Happens Where There is no Vision?

    How to Find your Vision

    How to Feed and Fight for Your Vision

Author's Final Words

Workbook and Journal

Introduction

Existing and living a fulfilling life that is truly worth living is a desire that every human being wants to achieve. Often times, we may feel that there is "something" missing in our lives. Well, the hard truth is that the missing "something" that many of us seek is a clear sense of our purpose in life.

Finding and achieving that purpose is actually a key to a better, happier, and more fulfilling life. However, to be able to find our purposes in life, we need to unlock our individual gifts. Yes, those valuable, waiting-to-be-discovered free gifts and talents that the Almighty God has blessed us with. Our gifts are the means through which we can get closer to our purposes in life.

Once we unlock those gifts, dreams, and talents, I believe that we can truly live our best lives with identified purposes. By so doing, our lives will also inspire, motivate, and encourage many other people to discover their purposes in life.

No matter your current age or your failures and wrong decisions in the past, you can still enjoy a truly worthy life. All you need is to unlock those hidden treasures within you and find your life purpose. Sound easy right? Well, it takes a lot of soul searching, commitment, consistency, and determination to achieve that feature.

In the name of being practical, most of us often take up "meaningless and socially befitting" jobs instead of committing our time, money, and energy to our personal development and growth. As a result, we slowly begin to grow hatred for these jobs. We constantly complain bitterly about the long hours of work, bosses' attitudes, coworkers, etc.

Deep within, we struggle with the lack of fulfillment in our lives and this leaves us searching for more. The reality is that these jobs are not aligned with our life purposes, as such; they distract us from finding the truth of our existence.

Of course, most of us are consciously aware that we don't fit in these jobs but we are too scared to step out of our comfort zones; personally, financially, and emotionally invest in something that we have almost no control over - our destinies, and build a life truly worth living. Well, embracing these things that each of us run away from and avoids in life is directly connected to finding our gifts and purposes in life.

When we fail to make time to identify and unlock the gifts that we have today, we run the risk of not sustaining the gifts we need for our life purpose in the future.

Interestingly, you don't have to go through any lengthy or expensive course to unravel more of this essential life knowledge of how to find your purpose. This book will be the ultimate guide on your journey to self discovery. Here, we'll be exploring the different stages that we all have to go through, to unlock our gifts; find and achieve our purposes as well as create fulfilling impacts on others.

All of the information provided in this book is based on the practical experiences of many who have learned a lot in their journeys of seeking their gifts and life purposes. The book is written to add value to your lives when applied and executed with purpose. At this point, I must emphasize that I am not a licensed therapist, psychologist, nor do I hold any certifications in this arena. However, I am chaplain, ordained minister, mentor and speaker serving communities across the world breathing life into my gifts and purpose, daily. A purpose that has taken me from a ten year tenure in the entertainment industry in Los Angeles, CA to a lifetime of service.

I am working with community, political, and influential leaders to develop programs, courses, and employment to make needful changes in the world. But it all starts with unlocking your gifts and finding purpose in life. I took to actionable steps that helped me unlock my gifts which led to me finding purpose along my journey.

It is my desire to help you along your journey. I wish you a delightful time while reflecting on the contents of this book!

CHAPTER 1

Assessing Who You are and the Person You are Becoming

> *One of the most powerful questions that you should ask yourself personally and professionally is, Who am I becoming?!*

In my commitment to taking this journey of self-growth with you, I've learned the importance of having a solid foundation in place. It will keep you standing with success and fulfillment, no matter the circumstance.

Every well-structured and long-standing building that you see has a very strong foundation. As someone on this journey of self-growth, you also need to have a solid foundation that can keep you standing with success and fulfillment, no matter the circumstance.

Self-reflection is an essential foundational stage that we must undergo to develop a more deliberate awareness of our purposes in life. It involves baring your souls; being brutally honest and diving into the deeper essence of who you are, your likes, dislikes, expectations, thoughts, behaviors, reactions to events, etc.

By reflecting on these things, you will be able to learn and understand who you are now, as well as identify the steps you need to take to live a more authentic and fulfilling life.

Interestingly, some of us sometimes don't realize that we have not unlocked our gifts or found our purposes in life because we are too busy catching up with life, with no time to reflect. Some of us also assume that we have found our purposes in life. As such, we keep running blindly on our life journeys to keep up with our so-called "dreams."

Sadly, we often end up crashing and burning out. You know why? We don't reflect on our lives! And that is a great recipe for disaster and failure.

Apart from the fact that failure can be very disheartening, it is often the start of a downward spiral that leads to extreme bitterness, shame, and self-loathing in our personal and professional lives. As emotional beings, when we fail to achieve certain life goals, we can quickly spiral downwards into a state of mental depression, coupled with negative beliefs and patterns of hopelessness. Unfortunately, it sometimes takes a long time for us to find our way out.

Let me give you a perfect example. Imagine you've attended the best schools, crushed competitive exams, obtained prestigious advanced degrees, and done every other thing that will make your future set for success, wealth, and happiness. While doing all of these, you never tried to reflect on who you are or embark on the journey of finding your true purpose in life.

Yet, you manage to acquire great academic and professional achievements, full-time better-paying jobs as well as get married with kids. However, you keep asking yourself, "Am I a big failure? Why is this so-called success not making me feel better? Why is making more money not fixing my lack of fulfillment?" And the most important question is; "How did I end up here?" You continuously find yourselves stacked with layers of fear and insecurities, feelings of dissatisfaction, dis-empowerment, resentment, and resignation.

Does that story sound similar to your life story right now? By now, I guess that you would acknowledge that your inability to engage in deep self-reflection is a recipe that inevitably pushes you further away from your gift and purpose in life. The journey to getting that fulfillment you desperately seek is NOT LINEAR!

Why Self Reflection is Needed to Unlock Your Gifts and Find your Purpose in Life

The benefits of introspection in the quest to find purpose cannot be overemphasized. The more you can make self-reflection a habit, the more you will enjoy the following benefits.

It enables self-awareness

Self-reflection creates for you an enabling environment to ponder on who you are, what you truly desire for your life as well as the areas of your life that are important to you like your family, work, love, and creativity. All of these soul-searching processes help you to understand yourself on a deeper level. As such, it becomes easier for you to unlock your God-given gift and to find your true purpose in life.

Also, greater self-awareness often equals better self-improvement. Ultimately, self-improvement is important for our well-being, as it helps us build and live our best lives. The beautiful thing about self-improvement is that it is something you can constantly improve. As such, it doesn't have to be one big gesture.

However, the results of investing everything you can into your self-improvement are definitely mind-blowing. You begin to experience joy in a way that you may have never felt before while laughing deeply from your soul and loving more passionately in every area of your life. When you improve the different aspects of your life, you just start to look at the world with a new lens.

It creates a greater sense of self

When you begin to know and connect with your soul on a deeper level, you get to enjoy a lot of power and a sense of inner calmness when tackling your everyday life situations. This, in turn, allows you to change your actions, thereby giving you a stronger sense of self that improves your confidence and level of self-esteem with increased knowledge and perspective. All of which contribute to unlocking your gift and finding your purpose in life.

Having a greater sense of self has a glow that many people oftentimes are attracted to. But they can't truly identify where it comes from. In my understanding, I believe it comes from living in your gift and walking in your purpose in life. Once you exist in your gift, you learn how to close old chapters in your life and embrace the new you which now shines very bright.

It improves decision-making

Unlocking your gifts and finding purpose in life is a continual process that involves making very important decisions that can make or mar your life forever. Fortunately, a personal reflection is an invaluable tool for getting stronger decision-making skills.

Additionally, it prepares you to become a stronger leader for the future, a well-balanced parent, a superior athlete, strengthening your ministry, and evolving as an entrepreneur. Decisiveness can sometimes be overwhelming when you're not walking in purpose. You second guess yourself and become timid in your decision making.

In times when you have to make a choice, self-reflection relieves you of unnecessary questioning, hesitation, and stress. The clarity of your thoughts makes the right choice clearer to you.

Help your true values

Our core values have great connections with our gifts and purposes in life. We'll discuss that more as we go further in this book.

However, we often need to take some quality time to sit, think, and figure out the guiding principles that we would desire to live by. Self-reflection is a means through which you get to know those core beliefs and feel more empowered to live by them.

Now that you know all of these benefits which make self-reflection an essential tool to unlock your gifts and discover your purpose in life, the next question you might ask is "How do I get started?"

How to Self-Reflect

Find quiet solitude

Indeed, our inner soul mostly speaks and reveals its wholeness under quiet, and calm environments and situations. To get quiet solitude for deep self-reflection, you can take advantage of nature like taking a walk to get some fresh air and clear your head, enjoying mountains and ocean views, doing beach runs, and watching the sunrise. This is how I connect to my inner peace and protect the gifts in my life.

When I identified my gifting, my priorities changed. The things that I valued before were no longer of any value to me and my purpose. Getting in nature at sunrise and/or sunset is how I avoid getting burnt out. It is my stress reliever and how I learn to refine my gift, daily. It's like musicians who have mastered their instruments at the highest level. They've committed to their craft and honor it by spending time refining it, daily. There's something about silence and being still in nature that has a calming effect on the soul.

Doing these kinds of activities at such time of the day when you are alone with just your thoughts and away from the chaotic lifestyles of the world. Often bring an inner peace that will help you to gain a strong connection with your soul. It helps you to break barriers over your life that you had no idea ever existed. It can make a difference between you unlocking your gift and finding your purpose or remaining the same forever.

Meditation

Sitting in silence for as long as you can and letting your mind wander may seem uncomfortable but believe it, it is very powerful! It is that moment when we take some time to sit silently without thinking about anything but rather listening to our minds, and our souls wholeheartedly whispering the full truth, about our lives in all ramifications, whether good or bad. In terms of meditation, gaining perspective on your life only takes a matter of giving yourself time and space.

When you make meditation a priority in your life, you unlock something deeper in your soul. You make room for your gifts to surface a lot easier. Purpose becomes part of your everyday life in everything you do.

Many people don't give meditation enough time to work wonders in their lives. If you learn to commit to it, you may find that it can be a contributing factor to unlocking your gift and finding lasting purpose.

Using a journal

Writing about your thoughts, feelings and daily activities significantly brings about new levels of understanding when you are reflecting on yourselves. A journal is like a sort of reminder that keeps everything about you in one place and enables you the opportunity to look back on your previous thoughts, beliefs, habits, a journey in life, personal development, personal growth, etc. All of which gives you a better understanding of who you were from the starting point as well as who you are becoming in terms of your growth.

Often times, what we write down comes true in life. Writing our goals, dreams, visions, thoughts, and anything that expresses the moment can leave a lasting imprint on our soul. We are evolving at a rapid pace in life and one way to track that pace is through journaling.

Journaling has a healing element that can change you. This is why I choose to journal daily without fail. When I committed to journaling everyday my life changed and my gift was refined.

Identify and ask important questions

To be able to reflect more deeply, you must question yourself daily on the "Why?" "What?" and Who?" Assess what you are grateful for in your life by writing it down.

Try to find answers to questions that matter to your soul like "Why do I act the way I act?" "Why do I think this way?" "Where do I want to get to?" "Who am I?" "Who am I becoming?" "Who do I want to be?" "Have I discovered my gift in life?" "Have I made an impact on anyone in the last 10 days?" And so much more!

I always say, "You have to become comfortable with being uncomfortable." So these questions may provoke some pinned up emotions. Let them come out and perhaps a breakthrough may occur. The point of this portion is for you to get real with yourself and DO THE WORK! Take your time to answer these questions and most importantly, be honest!

CHAPTER 2

Discovering Your Unique Gifts

> *We are all born with unique gifts as an offering to the world. These gifts manifested can inspire people, impact lives, and change the world. But it's up to us to manifest them.*

Right from a very young age, we are often told that each of us comes into this earth with a set of unique talents and special gifts that are of great essence to society. However, as many of us grow older, we begin to question if we hold any of such great uniqueness within ourselves, or even if we do, we struggle to figure out how to build these gifts into our lives; what vehicles to use to share our gifts with the world or the people we are compelled to share the gifts with.

Well, like we already established in the introduction of this book, we all have those unique gifts that are fueled by our deepest passions, which gives us an unwavering sense of purpose. But not everyone recognizes the special qualities and talents that they carry within themselves. The reason for this lack of self-awareness is that we are often oblivious to the things within and around us. Take for example, it may not always be obvious to you that your high level of intelligence or the things you have a natural flair for, may very well be the gift that you continuously seek.

Moreover, some of us keep struggling with finding fulfillment, direction, and meaning for different aspects of our lives, but we never stopped along the way to ask, "What is my gift?" Now is the right time to stop it all and start afresh!

Living in a world of uncertainty can be draining and suffocating while wondering if your gift is enough. Let's get you equipped with all the tools that you need for that eye-opening adventure!

How to Unlock Your Unique Gift

Discover the uniqueness within you

Your uniqueness simply means who you are in your most unapologetic and authentic form. Your uniqueness is what makes you stand out from others.

Of course, I know that being different can create uncomfortable feelings, as we live in a world that values sameness over uniqueness. But we must all understand that this uncomfortable feeling is only temporary.

To be able to unlock your gifts, you need to uncover and embrace your uniqueness. Your authentic attributes will help you to a great extent in figuring out what you have to offer. Do you remember those self-reflection exercises we discussed in the previous chapter? Now is the right time to use them!

To discover your uniqueness, you can revisit your childhood and connect with your inner child. The reason for this is that often as children we may harbor immense love for a certain activity or hobby but as we grow into adulthood, we are forced to let go of these fantasies because the world demands that we should be practical.

Think deep and find out - What are those things you do that put you completely at ease? What makes you feel secure? What matters most to you personally? What makes you very happy?

Trust me you'll discover several answers from your self-reflection exercises. Thus, you should take enough time to contemplate the thoughts from your inquiry and identify what things stand out for you as being your gift or strength among them. This is because it takes a lot to discover true passions, uniqueness, and talents that you can creatively explore and put to work for yourself and to make a positive impact on humanity as a whole.

Always remember that who you are is unique. So, when you think big and bold and share your uniqueness, you'll realize just how much the world needs you!

Eating is the last thing on your mind

For every one of us, there is something that makes us to jump out of bed before sunrise full of excitement. That same thing puts us in a "flow state" where we lose track of everything. It's like time passes by in the blink of an eye and eating is last thing on mind. There's a laser point focus that takes over us making us totally engaged.

Professional athletes, established actors, writers, and some elite content creators have mastered this process. Getting in their zone or flow state becomes 2nd nature for them. They're able to achieve levels of greatness surpassing many others in their chosen discipline. People like Serena Williams, Michael Jordan, Kobe Bryant (RIP), Denzel Washington, Viola Davis, and Shonda Rhimes have all mastered it in their careers.

Though for others, this thing might seem like a difficult deal, but it takes you only a little time and effort to achieve the best results. Figured it out already? Well, it's your passion and personal greatness!

Unlocking your gifts require you to ask yourselves these questions; "What can I do best with just little effort and time on my part?" "What lights me up and gets me totally motivated?" "What kinds of things do I enjoy doing so much that I lose track of time and those around me?"

Ask others

Figuring out your unique gift doesn't have to be a one-man job. You can always ask for insights from those who know you well or whom you spend the most time; like your family, friends, co-workers, or trusted advisors. Query them about your strengths, skills, and unique talents. Ask these things like, what makes me unique? What do you think I do particularly well? What is my strongest skill or characteristic?"

Trust me these special people sometimes get to observe you in ways that you cannot even observe yourself. Though they might give you exactly what you need, their opinions can be valuable and revealing clues for you.

Keep in mind that it is up to you to pay attention to the clues and apply them. Just having the information does nothing if you don't apply it. That makes the difference between the people who live in their purpose and have changed the world with their gifts.

Explore and never quit trying!

It is okay if you have numerous interests that you do not know which one of them can be your gift. All you have to do is explore your interests.

You can do this by taking up projects that relate to your interests, be it a writing project, coaching a soccer team, volunteering at church, organizing a friend's surprise birthday, etc.

You can then figure which of these interests gives you the most positive and joyful butterflies; decide which of these butterflies is your gift! Embrace those butterflies and develop that interest until it becomes a part of your being. But the key is to keep pressing on.

Can't unlock your unique gift at first? Keep pushing and going no matter what. It is always okay to take a break when you're burning out. However, don't quit. Giving up just after a few attempts simply means maybe it's not your gift. You need to keep trying because I promise you, you'll find it eventually.

Keep it at the back of your mind that once you identify your gift and figure out the most valuable way to use it, you get the opportunity to live your most fulfilling and richest life with a sense of purpose.

Why you need to unlock and use your gifts

Our gifts are like diamonds. In fact, they are our diamonds! It is a known fact that diamonds are attractive treasures that carry great value. Fortunately for us, diamonds (gifts) are everywhere. We just have to wake up and stop ignoring their existence. We have to dig them up; remove the dust and continuously polish them. By so doing, our diamonds will shine brighter and we may even get the chance to recognize more diamonds in our lives. When you invest immensely in your gift, the return of your investment is usually more than you can imagine. Besides, you actually have nothing to lose if you try.

If you are still not convinced of this "unlocking your gifts" thing, then I need you to know that I'm not giving up on you. I have some inspiring reasons to change your mind!

It expresses your deepest self

In case, you're still questioning yourself on whether you should step out of your comfort zone and unlock your gifts. I want you to understand these special diamonds are not just things you "do" with your time, rather they reflect who you are at a very core and deeper level, as well as who the world needs you to be. So ask yourself deeply, "Why should I deny my true nature and cause myself great misery?"

It fastens your personal growth

A great way to grow personally and professionally is to unlock your gift and find a way of building your life around this discovery. Finding the right gift for yourself and exploring different ways to increase its value can provide you with great riches in every aspect of our lives. If you would like to improve vastly, then start on where you are good at. Again, you have nothing to lose!

Impact and change other people's lives

As we grow up, we tend to benefit from the talents and gifts of other people; like Edison's light bulb, Zuckerberg's Facebook creations, even the enviable parenting and leadership skills of our parents and teachers. These gifts, no matter how small, contributed to our welfare in one way or another.

You might be wondering why I am telling you this. Well, I want you to understand that though these diamonds are your properties; they are not just for you but also to change the lives of others around us. It is a beautiful win-win game! Our gifts help us to help others.

When we identify our God-given gifts and tap from its energy of greatness, we may even positively influence a person's sense of belonging on earth. All of these can create a great and positive impact on our society at large.

It fosters internal satisfaction and fulfillment

Identifying, exercising, and sharing our gifts can make you feel whole and deeply fulfilled. On a personal note, I am more happy, focused, and optimistic when I am using my creative gifts. It makes me feel like me.

However, hiding your gifts to conform to a "more responsible and practical life," often brings misery in the end. You have to take in a huge breath and finally let go. Discovering and polishing your dreams will give you that measure of internal happiness and you know what? There is an extra bonus involved. This feeling of internal joy and satisfaction keeps you from seeking fulfillment and validation in empty vices, unhealthy distractions, addictions, and chaotic relationships.

You are allowed to outgrow people, places, and things. Remember you can't start a new chapter of your life if you keep rereading the last one.

Malik K. Murray

CHAPTER 3

Finding Your Purpose Path

"Why am I here on earth?" "What is my calling?" "What is my life work?" All of these questions point to the same thing - seeking your purpose in life.

Although we want to live a meaningful life filled with purpose, it can be very difficult to accomplish. Being intentional, patient, and aware will help you along your journey. The magic doesn't happen overnight.

Nevertheless, if you have executed the steps that we discussed in the previous chapter about unlocking your God-given talents and gifts, then I bring you good news - finding your purpose now may not be such a difficult task.

But don't celebrate just yet, we still have a long way to go because finding your purpose in life is not just an easy one and done task. So how does this treasure-hunting works? Let's find out!

Develop your strengths

Determining your strengths makes it easier for you to concentrate on where you have room for personal development. To find your purpose in life, you need to continuously invest time, energy, and maybe money in developing your strengths.

You may also need to work on improving your areas of weakness. By decreasing your areas of weakness and growing your strengths, you get to achieve the best results.

Take for example; you are extremely good at cooking, so to develop this strength, you can decide to try a new recipe to polish your culinary skills each week. That's how progress happens - practice makes perfect!

At this point, I must remind you that developing your strengths on a daily basis often requires you to leave your comfort zone. But trust me; the pain is totally worth it because, at the end of it all, you will enjoy a better sense of fulfillment and forward progress. So, let me ask you, how have you strengthened your gift in the last 14 days? Are you courageous and bold when it comes to developing your passion and gift?

Donate your gift to others

The act of service can change lives but most importantly, it will forever change yours.
- Malik K. Murray

It is a clear fact that when you donate your special gifts, talents, time, and energy to people or to a cause you care deeply about, you always receive more than what you gave. Believe me; you will be blown away by the incredible sense of joy and purpose that comes from sharing your gifts.

Your generosity can even boost your productivity, as such you don't only get to make a difference but you also gain more returns. If you really want to find out your true purpose in life, you can easily search for a cause that you care about and offer your services.

You have the voice of an angel but still struggle to find a sense of purpose; your neighbor invites you to come and sing for the kids at the orphanage during the weekend. That is your chance! Say that big YES today and thank me later!

You and your unique gift can make a great impact on someone's life. So, think, how have you made an impact on people's lives in the last 10 days? What would people say about you when you're not present?

Surround yourself with positive people

Though there is more to finding a purpose in life, positivity is a major influence. You need all the positivity that you can get!

If you really want to find a sense of purpose in life, being in a circle that is filled with people who are constantly in turmoil is definitely a No-No. Don't get me wrong, I'm not saying that those friends or co-workers are bad people. I just meant that they usually end up dragging you down with them and making you feel unmotivated.

Life is a hard game with enough obstacles already, so you can't afford any negative energy. You need to surround yourself around people whom you can freely share your fears and doubts. These are people who will listen to you, cheer you up, and fuel your fire and your desire to be a better person.

At this point, you should start picking out those loved ones who keep telling you, "Get back in there and do better! You can do it!" Keep them close because you'll need them.

Consult your values

To find your purpose in life, you need to understand and explore your core values. Why? You may ask. Well, your values are often the authentic representation of who you already are. Thus, when you take time to deeply consult and understand these values, it becomes easier for you to make your life decisions. Besides, living your life by honoring your core values creates deep contentment.

Now, you can make a list of your core values and use it as a guide for your quest of finding your purpose. Take, for example, if you value teaching children or expressing yourself through beautiful art or music, you can focus on that area and explore.

Find out - How are you honoring those listed values in your life right now? What information do your values give you about your calling?

Be patient

The bitter truth is that finding your purpose isn't something that happens overnight. It is a continuous, lifelong journey that requires taking one step at a time. In fact, there are cases where you may think you've gotten it all figured out, and it all changed in the blink of an eye.

You must internalize the virtue of patience and treat yourself with so much love and compassion along this journey of self-growth. Essentially, you must understand that though figuring out what your life calling is, takes some time, intentions, and efforts, but the end-gains makes it a well worthy journey.

CHAPTER 4

Finding Hope in Your Gifts and Purpose

Right from the first page of this book, I kept hammering on the fact that the journey to unlocking your gifts and finding purpose in life isn't an easy one. It's like a bumpy road that is filled with obstacles but also with success. Surely, you will get burnt out, mentally exhausted and emotionally drained at some point.

Still, you do not have to be discouraged because of these challenges. Remember that every problem comes with its solutions. Fortunately, this chapter is specially written to provide you with those solutions when it comes to finding hope in your gifts and life purposes.

We all need hope and optimism to get through those times when we feel lost. Finding hope can be a safe haven that you can live in while moving fast towards your success.

Hope isn't any strange magic that requires lots of exploration. It is always there in you, so you just have to find it. So how does this whole "hope" thing work?

Know where you are going and measure the gap

Ever heard of the statement, "You need to know where you're going to get there." Well, it means that having a vision (it doesn't have to be a specific idea), can help to maximize your hope.

Think about the kind of work you will be able to do and the great impact you will be making in the lives of other people around you. These thoughts might help you feel inspired and energized even in the face of the worst challenges ever.

Having gotten a vision in mind, you can measure the gap that stands in between you and the accomplishment of your vision, be it in terms of the knowledge, action, or experience you will need to get there.

Discipline yourself until changes come

You need to understand that your growth happens at the edge of your comfort zone. Many of us tend to create assumptions about ourselves and what we are capable of. However, changes often occur when we discipline ourselves to take a leap into a whole different world.

We need a great amount of self-discipline to be able to find hope in our gifts and purposes. So, challenge yourselves to grow!

Is there a community project that you can volunteer for that will improve your skills while helping to provide more purpose in your life? Is there a course you can take to keep learning and improving your talents? Get yourself entangled with those activities that will give you positive result and make your life one to be proud of.

Relax, Restructure, Refine, and Repeat

At some point in intense burnout, giving yourself space to rebuild is often the best action to take. Relax, eat, sleep - just take good care of yourself.

As you give yourself this space, try to objectively assess your previous actions that may have caused you to burnout. Use that information to restructure and refine your activities. It is okay to repeat the processes; all that matters is that you get your sense of purpose and fulfillment.

Find your support system

You don't have to go through the challenges of this journey alone. Intentionally building and maintaining a powerful support network will surely help you to find hope in your gifts and purpose. It may even challenge you to grow.

Find people who persistently see the bright side of things and soak up positive emotions from them. They could be your family, close friends, co-workers, mentors, or just someone who has an infectious smile and is always joyful.

Practice gratitude

Basically, being thankful can help you to discover that there are many reasons to be hopeful in your gifts and life purpose. Hence, you should count your blessings and remember your earlier miracles whenever you face any challenge that threatens your hope.

Force yourself to see all of those amazing achievements and know that you are more than capable of walking through the storm and victoriously coming out on the other side. Say this to yourself continuously, "It is absolutely possible for me to unlock my gifts and find my purpose in life."

Live with mindfulness

Mindfulness is an important tool that can help you to find hope in your gifts and purpose. It does not only help you to concentrate but also makes you more resilient.

Unfortunately, we live in a fast-paced world where the art of taking cognizance of our thoughts, actions, and reactions to events is absent. However, when you force yourselves to imbibe this virtue, you tend to learn from your past mistakes (rather than moan about them) and focus on making greater impacts with your future actions.

Though it sucks, the truth is that life happens whether we're prepared for it or not, it's up to us to focus on growth and personal development. Living with mindfulness helps us to stay in control of our reactions and to bounce back when things don't go the best way. Are you now convinced that you really need mindfulness to find immense hope in your gifts and purpose?

Fear will hold you back from becoming great. It steals the gifts and dreams that you've had since you were ten years old. Feel the fear and do it anyway.

Malik K. Murray

CHAPTER 5

Killing Every Fear

> *"Do the thing that you fear and the death of fear is certain."*
> *— Ralph Waldo Emerson*

Did you realize that I haven't mentioned "fear" throughout the previous four chapters? Well, if you have, then I know you might be thinking that I'm not human. However, far from it, I understand the powerful force that "fear" possesses. As such, this chapter is entirely dedicated to it.

From the first moment you make the decision to unlocking your gifts and finding your purpose in life, the ugly dragon will begin to surface. You will struggle to overcome that initial overwhelming fear of the unknown.

You might have started and given up on this journey several times because your fears keep giving you excuses that seem legitimate enough to make you to stop taking action and to crawl back to your comfort zone.

Though your fear is an evil subconscious tool that mentally limits and blocks you from achieving the life that you want, it can also be a beneficial compass that empowers you to make better decisions for yourself. The truth is that you don't have to be fearless to be able to find purpose in life.

This time needs to be different for you! You must not allow any of your fears to kill your hustle and belief before you even start progressing. This chapter is designed to give you all the help that you may need.

How to Overcome Your Fears

Understand and embrace your fears

To overcome your fears and achieve the life you want, you need to understand that you're not alone. Fear is an inevitable human emotion that lurks around.

Now that we have gotten that out of the way, try to identify your fears while being as specific as you can. You can say it out loud or write it in your journal.

By naming your fears and being consciously aware of them, you are forced to actually question and analyze why you are afraid; in the process, you gain the strength to deal with them.

However, the more you choose to ignore or hide your fears in the dark, the scarier they will be and the more disempowered you will become.

Be positive and visualize your success

Positive visualization is a mental mapping exercise that can help you to re-train your brain and free your mind from the strong clutches of fear.

To overcome the fear of failing while trying to unlock your gifts and find purpose, you need to visualize yourself going through the whole process and achieving great results. Take, for instance, you want to leave your current job and search for your purpose. You can conquer the fear of failure by imagining how your life will drastically change positively with more meaning after you succeed.

This positivity ensures that when your body moves, it is more likely to follow that pre-ordained path that you have always imagined.

Just do it!

Do you know that action helps to eliminate fear while inaction and procrastination feed it? I know this might sound strange but you need to know that whatever your fear, it is most likely what you should be executing direct massive actions on. So why don't you go for it?

Let your fear drive you to take the best actions. Even when you can hear that voice whispering about how you're going to fail, still take action! Remember that it takes willingness, hard work, and determination to overcome your fears and succeed in life.

I will also recommend that the moment you begin this journey of personal development, you build the highest level of excitement. Be excited that you have gotten a promising chance to change your life and create a life that you truly desire for yourself.

This will fire up your energy. As such, instead of you to be scared about the length or challenges of the journey, you get thrilled about it. This may help you to stay focused and determined all through.

Believe in yourself

Let me put this as nice as possible, "If you don't believe in yourself or you engage in self-sabotage, then you will not get that desired self-fulfillment that you seek." You need to dig deep and build that trust and confidence within yourself.

If you want a different and fulfilling life then you need to do things differently. I'm not insinuating that you should become someone you are not. What I mean is, you need to improve your self-esteem because your fears are not going to go away without that boost in your self-confidence.

When you build confidence and discipline yourself to do that thing that scares you, then your fear diminishes and your self-esteem rises beyond expectation.

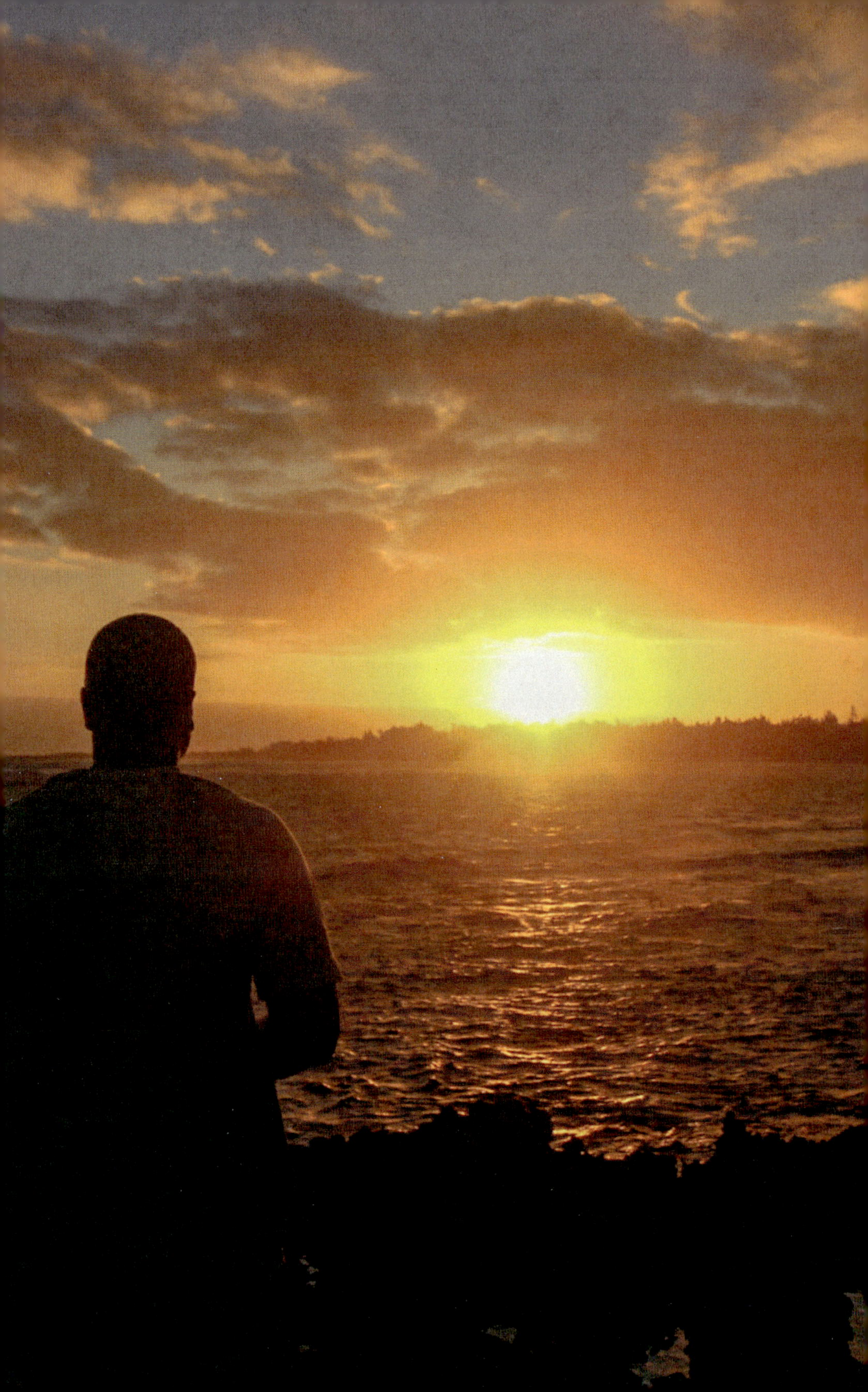

CHAPTER 6

Holding On To Your Vision

> *"Work without vision is drudgery and vision without work is a tragedy."*
> - Bertha Hicks-Taylor

Like I stated previously, in order to begin your journey of self-growth and discovery, you will need to unlock your gifts and find your purpose in life.

How you achieve this transformation is solely up you. The question that I will ask you specifically is, how bad do you desire growth? Think about It, you have passions, values, cultural, and spiritual beliefs that dictate how you live life.

All in which may have a powerful impact on your life and many others. I'd like to submit for your consideration that perhaps, this is a form of purpose. Although unrecognized, untapped, and clearly unrealized. You have purpose within your life. Which leads me to the purpose of this chapter, do you have a clear vision?

At this point, I need you to ask yourself, "Do I have a clear vision of what I want for my life?" Is it to finally build my dream business or a beautiful new home? Is it to find a fulfilling career or an incredible romantic partner?

Having a clarified vision is a powerful and effective strategy that can help you to achieve your purpose in life. It is like a compass that guides you to make the best decisions; all of which propel you toward your best moment in life. Your vision is an active and ongoing dream that you are striving to achieve. It projects a clear image of a possible destination, thereby pulling you forward and giving you extra enthusiasm and energy to strive courageously toward fulfilling your life purpose. In short, when you live by your vision, everything changes for good!

Unfortunately, some of you might strongly believe that intentionally creating a vision for your lives is a frivolous and fantastical waste of time and energy. But if you ask me, "What happens if I don't have the vision to hold on to?" Brethren, I have scary answers to that question! Let's get right into it!

What Happens Where There is no Vision?

Permit me to state this crystal clear, "If you don't have vision, you are walking majestically on the path of catastrophe." Without a clear vision statement for your life, you are most likely to struggle with boredom and mediocrity.

As human beings, we often need a sense of direction to feel fulfilled, purposeful, and satisfied. However, individuals with no vision lack this sense of direction, as such; they end up wandering and being unsure of where they are going. Basically aiming at a non existent target.

Having much less energy and passion for life is a distinct quality of vision-less people. Are you still wondering why your full-time better paying job is monotonous or why all your relationships feel completely shallow? Let me remind you again; it's because you don't have a clear image of your vision.

By not having a vision for your life, you are not only denying yourself a beautiful and fulfilling life, but you are also cheating the part of humanity that needs to tap greatness from your life when you live fully in your gifts, passions, talents, and dreams.

At this point, I'm certain that some of you might have been coming up with excuses to justify the lack of vision in your lives - distractions of life, fears, lack of knowledge on how to discover your vision, etc. Honestly, all of these are real problems that need to be taken care of. However, these excuses should not be hindrances in any way. You need to understand that most of the worlds greatest heroes like, Steve Jobs, Mother Theresa, Nelson Mandela, and Dr. Martin Luther King all lived a fulfilling and purposeful life with the help of their compelling visions.

You've read those horrible consequences that we discussed earlier. Don't let them happen to you. You deserve so much better! So, this is the best time for you to grow up, take responsibility, invest in yourself and do anything else it takes to find your vision. I can't promise you that it is going to be an easy task but I know that you will surely be laughing deeply from your soul when the process is all over.

Whew! That was a lot of harsh revelations! If you are ready to conceive that powerful life map from within, then I'd really love to help you. So, let's get started on this vision seeking adventure!

How to Find your Vision

Where there is no vision, the people will perish.

Before we get started on discussing the steps to discovering your life vision, I want to emphasize that a large part of this discovery is a spiritual experience that demands intense introspection. Now, how does it work?

Get ready to reflect

Finding a quiet place that will enable you to stay focused and take this exercise very serious is a great way to get started. It is also important that you do away with anything that might distract you; turn off your phone, laptops, and any other electronic devices in your possession. You can also try out some of the options we listed in the first chapter of this book. Just make sure that you do things that can help you to feel at peace and be creative

Create your dream list

Once you are all settled, get your pieces of paper and begin to explore your deepest desires and dreams. Asking yourselves thought-provoking questions like "What do you want? What issue do you want to solve? What kind of freedom do you want to have? What do you want your life to look like in 5 years? What do you want your family to look like? What would you tlike your career to be? Where do you want to go?" - Can help you to discover what you really want out of life.

Though these questions might sound deceptively simple, they are often the most difficult to answer. The secret key here is to free your mind and let it go wild. Envision what you want your life to look like; imagine every possibility and dream with reckless abandon!

Write down every thought without any form of restraint. You don't need to analyze anything. Just go with the flow and write! In this paper, everything you write is possible. To create an exciting and compelling vision, you have to give yourself the freedom to dream. Use your imagination to feel and create vivid pictures of what does not exist yet.

While creating this dream list, you must consider every aspect of your personal and professional life: your family, career, personal development, health, quality of life, spirituality, relationship, and even the fun part.

Analyze and find the common subject

Now that you are done with exploring your dreams, the next thing is to take up your list and start drawing out common themes. What do I mean? Find out what subjects, words, phrases, sentences or themes that keep coming up over and over.

Then, consider which of these common subjects gives you butterflies inside or gets you overly excited and passionate. Now write those themes down separately on a different piece of paper.

Write a vision statement and list your action steps

Now you need to be as creative as possible, by thinking of a one or two-sentence statement that encapsulates the common themes that you have separated in the previous step. It needs to be as specific as possible. Also, ensure that your personal vision statement is compelling enough to move you on a deeper level.

To help you get started on working on your vision, you can write down about five action steps that you will focus on to get closer to reaching your dream destination. The idea here is that when you have accomplished those action steps, you can come up with new ones.

Make your vision statement accessible

You need to be constantly exposed to your vision statement. This is because it takes time to reshape your thoughts and focus.

Now you can write your vision statement in your journal or place them on your phones so that you can read it anywhere and at any time. You could even make copies to place by your bedside, in your office, living room, or any other convenient places for easy access.

Be patient and flexible

Your newly-discovered vision is a work in progress that demands patience. It requires refinement and clarity to deliver favorable results.

Hence, you should be open to the fact that your vision may need changes as time goes on or as your circumstances become different. All you have to do is to think reasonably and make changes when you feel necessary.

Feeding and Fighting for Your Vision

Finding your vision is a stepping stone to the accomplishment of your dreams. So I say, "A big congratulations on making it this far." But we still have more to do.

The next tough question is, "Do you have what it takes to hold on to your beautiful vision in the face of doubt and challenges?"

Take your mind back and try to recall if you have ever been told that what you wanted for your life was impossible; or that your dreams weren't just for you because you are incapable. If yes, do you remember how those comments sowed the seed of doubt in you and kept you feeling and acting small?

Why am I asking all these questions? That's because I need you to be prepared for similar situations to reoccur as you move ahead in this journey of unlocking your gifts and finding your purpose in life. Basically, we all struggle with dark moments of doubt, failure, and other forms of negativity at some point in our life journeys. It's an inevitable stage we all have to go through.

But there is a good side to these sad tales and that is the fact that with persistence, we can eventually emerge victoriously. Your vision is yours to foster; hold on to and take action towards making it a reality.

If your vision is something that you deeply desire for the betterment of your life and, if you truly believe you are worthy of achieving and getting it, then I say this with utmost belief and confidence, "You will surely turn that vision into a reality. "You don't believe me? Well, get ready to be shocked!

How to Feed and Fight for Your Vision

First, I need you to see your vision as a living thing from your heart that gets hungry and needs to be protected. The subtitle makes more sense now, right? As you pursue your visions and dreams, challenges are bound to come. Fortunately, I have some secrets to overcoming these challenges.

Move on from your past

Many of us allow our past mistakes, defeats, or failures to hold us from realizing our vision. To fight for your new life vision, you need to let your wounds heal fully; let your past go, live in the present, and see how bright your tomorrow is.

Of course, you can always use your past experience to improve your future today. Just don't waste your precious time and energy being stuck in the past. We need that time and energy for something bigger - to build your new vision into a mind-blowing reality!

Never stop believing in yourself and your vision

Pursuing your vision demands that you have a strong belief in yourself. I know that we all have the potential to be a trailblazer, trendsetter, and real difference-maker. All it takes to unleash them is our beliefs and actions.

Honestly, as you are actively chasing your vision, it may feel like you're waiting for an eternity to experience clarity. Then you may start to downplay or disqualify your vision. Please don't do that! You should understand that pursuing your vision and creating a meaningful life takes time and effort.

You need to keep reminding yourself that your vision and dreams are worth believing in. In fact, you are worth the effort to visualize how powerful and exciting the realities of your visions will be.

Be open to changes

Change is a constant thing that you have to embrace when pursuing your vision in life. Your ability to feed and fight for your vision is greatly influenced by your willingness to break free from unnecessary comfort and explore new and innovative ways of accomplishing things. At some point, you might have to change your inner circle of influence. As mentioned earlier your mindset will determine how well you adapt to change. Your circle of influence plays into your personal development and who you are becoming. What books are you currently reading? Who's voice are you listening to the loudest? Where do you spend most of your time? All of these things matter a lot.

Now don't be quick to assume that I'm asking you to change your unique self. No that's not what I mean. Changing the direction of your life often requires that you drop certain bad habits or attitudes for you to grow well and fight for the vision that you strongly believe in.

Be well-informed before you make decisions

To feed your vision and keep it protected until it is finally realized, you must ensure that you don't rush into making quick decisions. It can cost you many years of agony.

Surely, there will be times when those around you will give limited information and try to influence you to make decisions based on their words. Please fight for that vision of yours! You need to take a step back and do your homework. Spend quality time to research and gather enough reliable information so that you can easily make a sound and well-informed decision.

Be positive.

Being constantly attacked with relentless negative thoughts and an overwhelming sense of fear and doubt is a challenge that you must overcome while pursuing your visions. Acknowledging these difficulties is a great way to start. Once you know your problem, you can begin to search for where to tap positivity from.

A positive mindset helps to you hold on firmly to your vision until it is realized. But positive thinking isn't magic, rather it needs to be developed over time. You can start by focusing on finding the proverbial silver lining in every cloud, practicing positive self-talk, reading motivational books, starting every day with a positive note. Positive thinking can help you to fight for and hold on to your vision for as long as possible. In fact, it can completely transform your life for the better.

Holding On To Your Vision

Walk in faith and stand firm

If you really want to realize your vision in every area of life, then you must develop an unstoppable attitude. Even when people including your family, friends, and even strangers, laugh at your "unrealistic" dreams, or express their opinions on how you can never attain what you strive for, you must hold on firmly to your vision and trust the process. Believe me, you don't need anybody's permission to dream big and achieve your goals in life. You have every right to live your best life with purpose.

It is okay to fall or fail sometimes while trying. However, the most important thing is to keep picking up the pieces of your vision after you drop them. After you go through your periods of doubt and of fear, you must fight hard to go back to your original vision.

The knowledge that we will eventually attain our goal can help us to gain internal strength to stand upright and continue running after a fall, no matter how terrible. If after having our moments of doubt and disappointment, we can regroup and get back on our original path, then we are not just strong fighters but also inspiring winners.

Certainly, there are times when the darkness of the night makes us believe that there will be no daylight. However, if we choose to walk in faith and hold on for just a little bit longer, then at some point, the new day will come. It's always darkest before dawn. But remember there is always light at the end of every dark tunnel.

Remember why you started this and what it will cost you if you quit

It is very easy to forget why you are pursuing a particular vision when difficulties and challenges arise. This explains why we stated earlier that you should make your vision statement very accessible. A constant reminder of why you are taking certain actions might give you insurmountable strength to fight for your vision and feed your hunger for achieving your goals in life. Reminding yourself of your life purpose might also help you to hold on firmly until your vision is realized

Another effective strategy that might give you plenty of reasons to fight for your vision is to occasionally remember what it might cost you if you quit. I know this might sound quite harsh but I promise you, that it will deliver great results.

Think about how a big part of your life will be lost if you quit pursuing your vision, how you will miss living a great and fulfilling life, how you will forfeit personal and professional growth, and how you will lose your sense of direction. You can even shut your eyes firmly and try walking to a particular point. You'll surely keep hitting walls or some other things. That's exactly what is in store for you if you quit chasing your distinct vision. These harsh realities will ensure that we continue to hold within our hearts our vision -- whether for ourselves or humanity as a whole.

I know you might be feeling overwhelmed at how much work you need to do! Just take a deep breath and calm down. I need you to know that You Can Do This and that is all that matters.

I'm cheering you on to believe that your vision matters and it will surely transform your life and the lives of so many people that are waiting for you to live your destiny! So find it, feed it and fight for it!

Jeremiah Bostwick Photogrpahy

Author's Final Words

> *Sometimes you just need to take one step backward to make ten steps forward in the right direction. Never be ashamed of starting over in life.*

Have you ever wondered what it felt like to wake up in the morning feeling overly excited and jumping out of bed with a thirst to impact others and truly make a difference? Well, your gifts and purposes are the ultimate keys that you need to get that incredible amazing lifestyle.

It has been a great pleasure having you take this beautiful journey of intense revelation. In this book, you have been exposed to a lot of powerful tools that can help you unlock your gifts and find your purposes in life. However, reading the contents of this book is just the beginning, you must make time to reflect deeply on its life lessons and inculcate them into your daily lifestyle.

As you begin your quest to unlock your gifts and find your life purpose, I want you to know that I strongly believe in you because you were born to live a beautiful and meaningful life!

Unlocking your gifts and finding your purpose will undoubtedly give you the power to shape your destiny. When you find what you're looking for, you'll definitely feel it deep down in your bones, and believe me, it is a whole new feeling of fulfillment! So, I say to you, "Dare to win and take a chance!"

A Special Dedication

This book is also dedicated to my father William Murray Jr. (Pops aka Poppy) who left us in July 2015 to pursue a higher purpose for the Lord. Pops, I want to start by saying, thank you. Thank you for all of the unspoken lessons that you taught me growing up in Philly when I was just a curious young man. You showed me the meaning of showing up as a father no matter how flawed I am.

For that I am truly grateful. I hope to have at least 5% of your work ethic, spirit, and dedication to your family. You set the standard extremely high as a father. Just so you know I'm still working on becoming a better fisherman.

Mr. Eric Joseph (Grampy) I want to thank you for teaching me how to live life on my own terms and how to enjoy life as it comes. When you met my pop before he left the world, he truly appreciated your zeal for life. It inspired him to enjoy life again. Thank you for impacting me in such a profound manner and leaving such a very strong legacy to the world.

Rest well, party hard, and thank you both for helping us all unlock our gifts and finding true purpose in life.

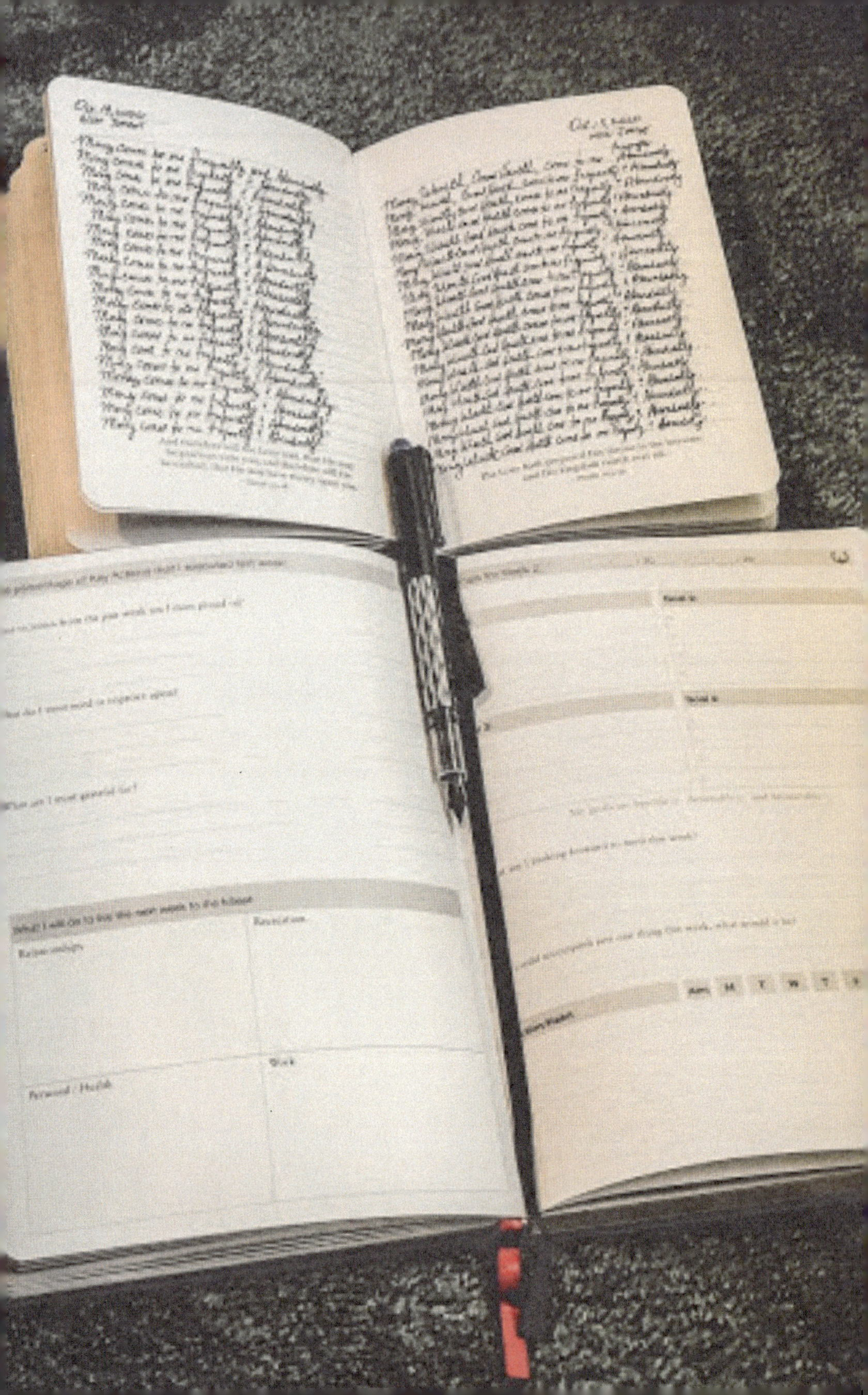

Workbook and Journal

Journaling is the one thing in my life that has truly transformed me from the inside out. Through journaling I've found my purpose, myself, and my gift. It is my hope that you find your purpose path through journaling.

Journal

Work Book: Try to find answers to questions that matter to your soul.

Who am I?

_____
_____
_____
_____
_____
_____
_____
_____
_____
_____
_____
_____
_____
_____
_____
_____
_____
_____

Workbook and Journal

Journal

Work Book: Identify and ask important questions. You must be honest for this to work.

Who am I becoming?

Journal

Work Book: Discover the uniqueness within you.

What are those things you do that put you completely at ease?

_____

_____

_____

_____

_____

_____

_____

_____

_____

_____

_____

_____

_____

_____

_____

_____

_____

_____

Journal

Work Book: Your uniqueness is unapologetic and authentic.

What matters most to you personally?

_____
_____
_____
_____
_____
_____
_____
_____
_____
_____
_____
_____
_____
_____
_____
_____
_____
_____
_____

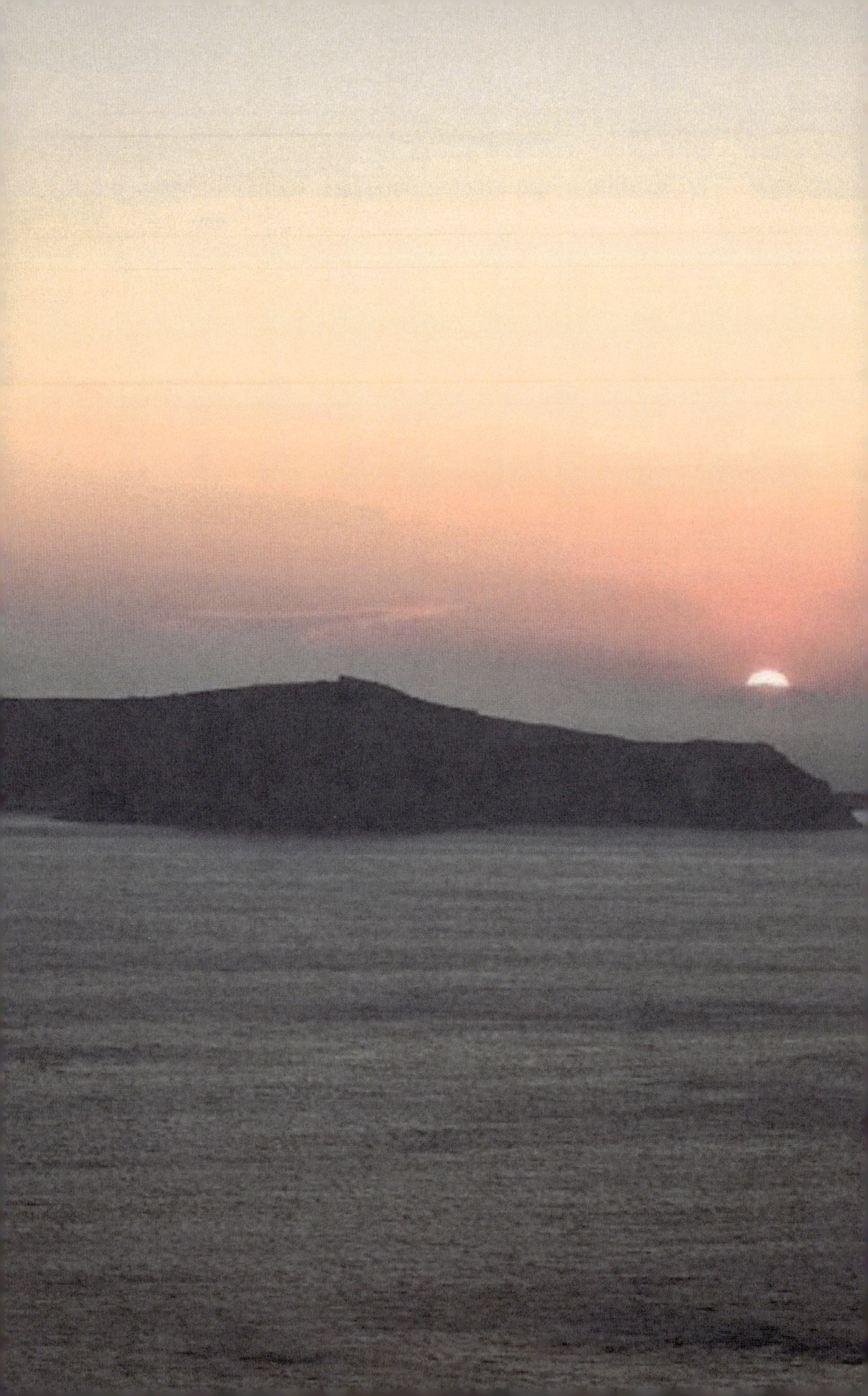

Journal

Work Book: Identify your passion and personal greatness

What can I do best with just little effort and time on my part?

_____
_____
_____
_____
_____
_____
_____
_____
_____
_____
_____
_____
_____
_____
_____
_____
_____
_____

You are halfway through this exercise. Don't quit on yourself. Remember why you starting this journey in this first place. This workbook and journal is for you. You will benefit from it once it's complete. Let's go!

Journal

Work Book: Identify your passion and personal greatness

What kinds of things do I enjoy doing so much that I lose track of time and those around me?

_____

_____

_____

_____

_____

_____

_____

_____

_____

_____

_____

_____

_____

_____

_____

_____

_____

_____

Journal

Work Book: Ask Others- Figuring out your unique gift doesn't have to be a one-man job.

What makes me unique?

What is my strongest skill or characteristic?"

_____

_____

_____

_____

_____

_____

_____

_____

_____

_____

_____

_____

_____

_____

_____

Workbook and Journal

Journal

Work Book: Ask others

What do you think I do particularly well?

What makes me very happy?

Journal

Work Book: Finding your purpose path.

Why am I here on earth?

What is my calling?

What is my life work?

_____

_____

_____

_____

_____

_____

_____

_____

_____

_____

_____

_____

_____

_____

_____

_____

_____

_____

Journal

Work Book: Discipline yourself until changes come.

Do I have a clear vision of what I want for my life?

Is it to finally build my dream business or a beautiful new home?

Is it to find a fulfilling career or an incredible romantic partner?

_____

_____

_____

_____

_____

_____

_____

_____

_____

_____

_____

_____

_____

_____

_____

_____

_____

Day #1

How has this book impacted your life?

Workbook and Journal

Day #2

What have you learned from journaling & meditation?

_____
_____
_____
_____
_____
_____
_____
_____
_____
_____
_____
_____
_____
_____
_____
_____
_____
_____
_____
_____
_____
_____

Day #3

Write down one thing that are you committed to changing over the next 10 days?

_____

_____

_____

_____

_____

_____

_____

_____

_____

_____

_____

_____

_____

_____

_____

_____

_____

Malik K. Murray
@Malikkmurray

Never let people steal your joy. No matter how close they are to you. Protect your inner peace ✌🏽

Day #4

What is holding you back from starting a new business?

Day #5

How has your mindset changed in the 7 days?

You only have one life to live and this is your time to embrace your gift and walk in your purpose in life. Tomorrow will never come and yesterday is a distant memory when it comes to life. You have this moment in time to achieve the things that you've always desired in life. I hope this book provided you with a little clarity as to what's next in life.

Keep refining your gift and walk tall in your purpose.

Your friend and mentor,

Malik K. Murray

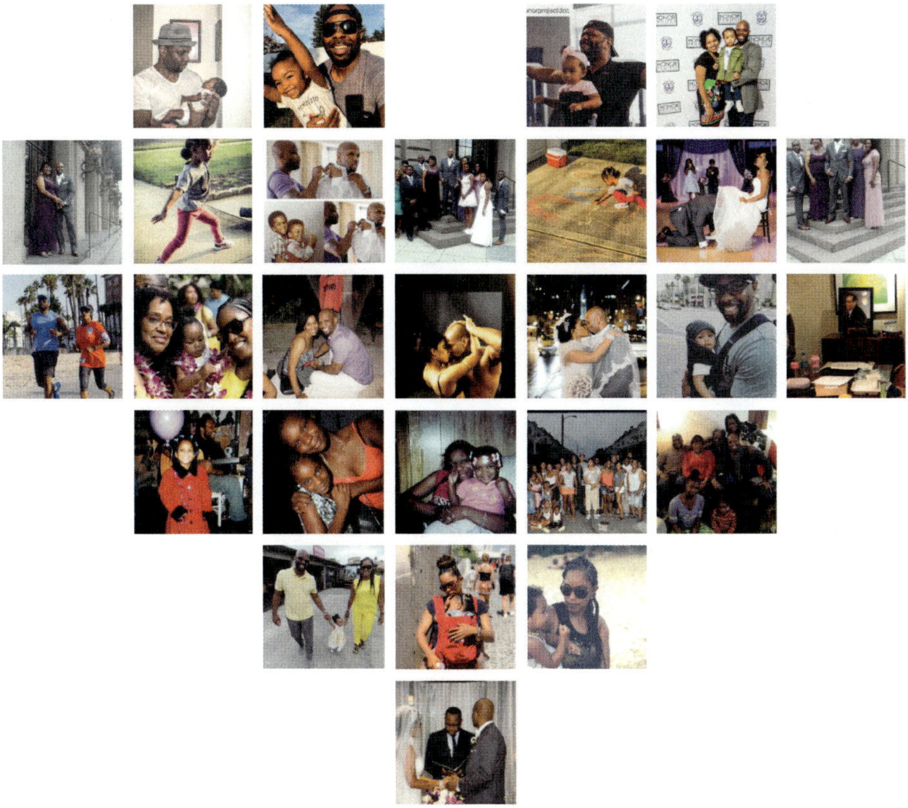

Thank you Ma Dukes for believing in me and always supporting my dreams. Love ya!

Made in the USA
Middletown, DE
10 October 2022